God and His Word Crafts and More

(Grades 2–6)

Written and Illustrated by Becky Radtke

Cover Illustrated by Corbin Hillam

Unless otherwise indicated, the New International Version of the Bible was used in preparing the activities in this book. Scripture taken from the HOLY BIBLE, NEW INTERNATIONAL VERSION. Copyright © 1973, 1978, 1984 International Bible Society. Used by permission of Zondervan Bible Publishers.

Table of Contents

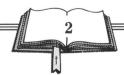

SS48838

To Parents and Teachers

It's so important that children learn at an early age who God is and all about His Word. With so much information to convey, it can be hard to know where to start. That's where this book is helpful! Filled with crafts, games, songs, and puzzles, it can assist you in revealing to children the wonders, qualities, and deep love of God in an exciting and stimulating way.

Each activity features valuable information about God, His Word, and His love for us. Discuss the information presented with the children and be sure to go over the activities with them as many will require your input.

All materials needed are listed for each activity and should be easily accessible. Any patterns called for are included. Step-by-step, easy-to-follow directions are also given and are written to the children.

However, use your judgment on when to take over and perform tasks that you feel may be potentially dangerous (like cutting, handling glass jars, etc.) for younger or challenged children. Encourage and cheer the children on as they participate in a game or song, or strive to solve a puzzle!

As you journey through this book, do your best to radiate enthusiasm as you teach the exciting truths of God and His Word to impressionable minds and eager ears!

SS48838

Our Lord Lives

(bookmark)

Isn't it comforting to know that we are worshipping the one true and living God? And what joy we can experience when we realize that He deeply loves and cares for each one of us! Use this large, shiny number one as a bookmark and let it be a symbol of these wonderful truths!

Materials Needed:

bookmark pattern
3" x 4½" piece of white tagboard
3" x 4½" piece of aluminum foil
three 4" strips of crepe paper
tape
pencil
scissors

Directions:

1. Cut out the bookmark pattern, lay it on the tagboard, and use a pencil to trace around it.

2. Carefully cut it out.

3. Wrap and tape the aluminum foil around the front and back of the tagboard.

4. Cut a small slit at the inner inside point as shown. This will create a tab that can be secured onto a book page.

5. For a festive touch, tape the crepe paper strips onto the bottom of your new bookmark!

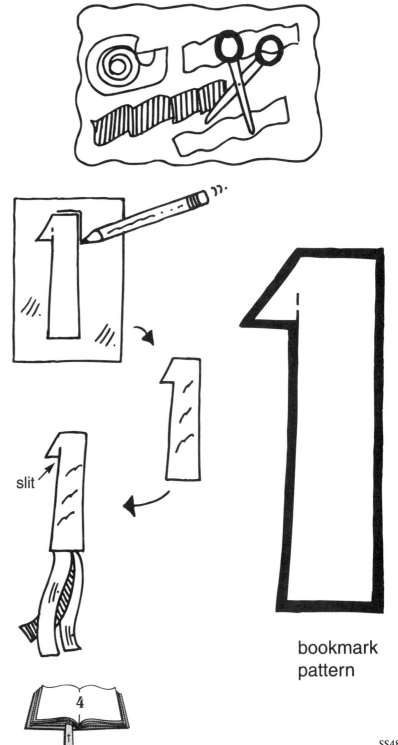

slit

bookmark
pattern

4

SS48838

Only One God

(rainbow reminder)

No matter what you hear, read, or see, it is important to remember th[...]
living God. The Bible says that God is the Alpha and the Omega. That means that [...],
circular lid used in this craft, has no beginning or end. Hang your completed rainbow reminder on
a window where sunlight can shine through it. Each time you pass it, let it remind you of the
awesome God we serve!

Materials Needed:

large, clear, plastic coffee can lid; markers; yarn; gold or silver sequins; hole punch; small suction
cup with hook; string; glue; scissors

Directions:

1. Use different colored markers to make large, horizontal stripes across the top of the lid.

2. Punch a hole near the top edge.

3. Glue a length of yarn around the entire outside edge.

4. Use glue to write the word "God" in capital letters as shown.

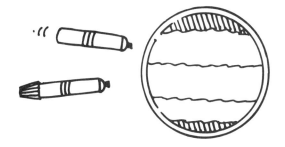

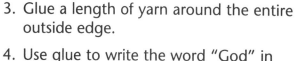

5. Carefully place pieces of yarn over the glue letters and let dry.

6. Randomly glue some sequins on the lid to add some sparkle.

7. Slip a length of string through the hole and knot securely to make a loop.

8. Proudly hang your creation from the hook attached on the suction cup!

SS48838

Let's Spell It Out

(puzzle)

Our world offers many types of gods. We must be careful not to be tricked or led to believe in any of them. The Bible, answers to prayers, and the changes God makes in our hearts are proof that our Lord is the only real God worthy of praise. Get set to create a picture that will clearly spell out this truth!

Materials Needed:

picture puzzle pattern, crayons, various colors of glitter, newspaper, glue

Directions:

1. Color the picture according to this code: all black dots—blue; all triangles—red; all hearts—green; all squares—purple.

2. Smear glue over all of the remaining letters—those with no symbol in them. They will spell out the name of the One we worship!

3. Carefully sprinkle glitter onto these letters so this name really stands out from the rest of the page. Gently shake the extra glitter onto the newspaper.

4. Hang your masterpiece in a high traffic area. Be ready to explain its meaning to anyone who asks!

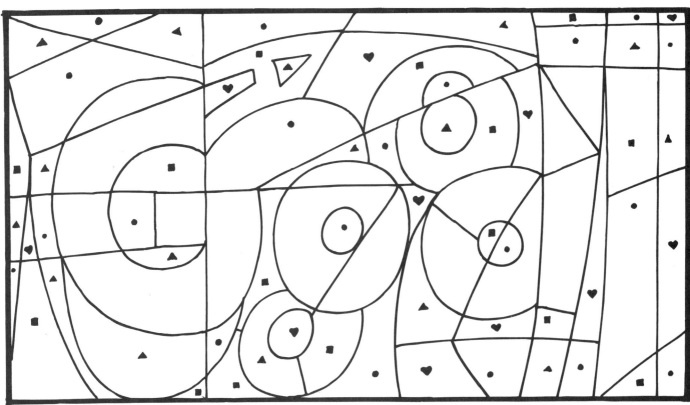

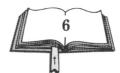

SS48838

Pick and Choose

(bracelet)

Because God is alive and powerful, He can perform miracles, change circumstances, and listen to us when we pray. No other gods do any of these things. The bracelet you will be making will have only one white bead on it. This will represent God. The black ones will represent false gods. Each time you wear your bracelet, think of what the colors of the beads stand for.

Materials Needed:
black beads (with holes), one white bead (with hole), yarn or thin twine, scissors

Directions:

1. Take a long piece of yarn or twine and wrap it so that it fits loosely around your wrist. Add about four inches to this length and cut.

2. Tie a knot(s) at one end of the yarn, leaving about a 2" tail. This is so the beads will not slip off.

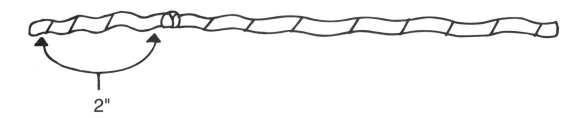

2"

3. String the beads onto the yarn. You can place the white one wherever you wish. (You might want to add an extra knot after each bead for a special look.)

4. When you are finished stringing the beads, tie another knot(s) to hold them in place, leaving another 2" tail.

5. Place your creation around your wrist and tie the two tails together to finish your stunning bracelet!

7

SS48838

Super Seasons

(shoebox)

We only need to take a quick look around to figure out that our mighty Creator, God, made all that we see. Such beauty, order, and balance could never have just happened. When we notice the changing seasons, we can be reminded of this. God wants us to enjoy each season. Make a shoebox that will hold special nature items that you can collect during all four seasons!

Materials Needed:

shoebox (medium to large), blue construction paper, variety of decorative items that will add a three-dimensional effect (cotton balls, craft sticks, milk caps, straws, bits of yarn, etc.), crayons, markers, glue, scissors

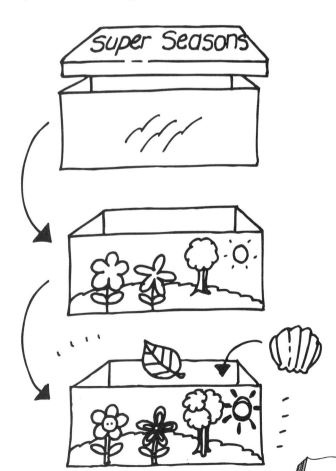

Directions:

1. Measure, trim, and glue blue construction paper to cover the top lid and all four sides of the shoebox. (You do not need to cover the bottom.)

2. Use crayons or markers to write "Super Seasons" on the top of the lid.

3. Think of a fall, winter, spring, and summer scene. Then draw one on each side of the box.

4. Choose and glue any of the items onto your scenes to give them a three-dimensional look. You could use bits of cotton for snow, straw for tree branches, a milk cap for the moon or sun, small pieces of yarn for rain, etc. Be creative!

5. Each time you are outdoors, keep an eye out for small things that you find attractive—flowers, leaves, shells from the beach, or pretty stones. When you return home, place them in your Super Seasons shoebox for safe keeping!

8

Intricate Insects

(pompon bugs)

Aren't you glad God made insects? There are so many different kinds! It's great fun to discover their different sizes, shapes, and colors. They are also fascinating to watch. Have you ever spent a few minutes watching ants build a hill, or seen a ladybug spread its bright, red wings as it gets ready for flight? Insects are truly remarkable creatures that God created. Today, you will have the chance to create your favorite insect, or you can even make up one of your very own!

Materials Needed:

books on insects
variety of colored pompons
   (small and medium-sized)
set of wiggly eyes
white paper
scraps of felt
black pipe cleaners
glue
scissors

Directions:

1. Look through the insect book and decide which one you would like to create. Or, if you prefer, you can think one up!

2. Use the materials provided to assemble your chosen bug. Use pompons for the body parts, white paper for wings, and pipe cleaners for legs and antennae. Use felt scraps to make mouths, spots, or markings.

3. Let your creature dry completely. Then choose a special place to display your handiwork!

9

SS48838

Fabulous Flowers

(game)

Nature is full of beauty! It is one way that we know that God is real. Some of the most lovely examples of nature are flowers. They come in such a dazzling array of colors and give off so many pleasant scents. Remember to thank God each time you pass a garden filled with them. Note: Two to four players work best for this game.

Materials Needed (per player):

game board and game pieces on page 11, tagboard (a little larger than the game board), crayons, glue, scissors, an envelope (one per group of players)

Directions:

1. Cut on the dotted lines to separate the game board and the game pieces.

2. Color the game board and then glue it onto the tagboard. After it has dried, trim off the excess tagboard.

3. Cut on the solid, thick, black lines to separate the game pieces. Place them all into an envelope. All other players should put their game pieces into the envelope at this time also.

4. You will need at least two players. Let the first player pull (without looking) a game piece from the envelope. He or she will then use the piece to cover the matching letter on his or her game board. The next player should do the same.

5. When a player draws a game piece and the corresponding letter has already been covered on the board, he or she should discard it by placing it onto the flowerpot area.

6. Whoever covers all the letters to spell "flower" first is the winner! If you are playing with three or four players, the group may wish to continue to see who comes in second and third.

SS48838

Fabulous Flowers

(game) continued

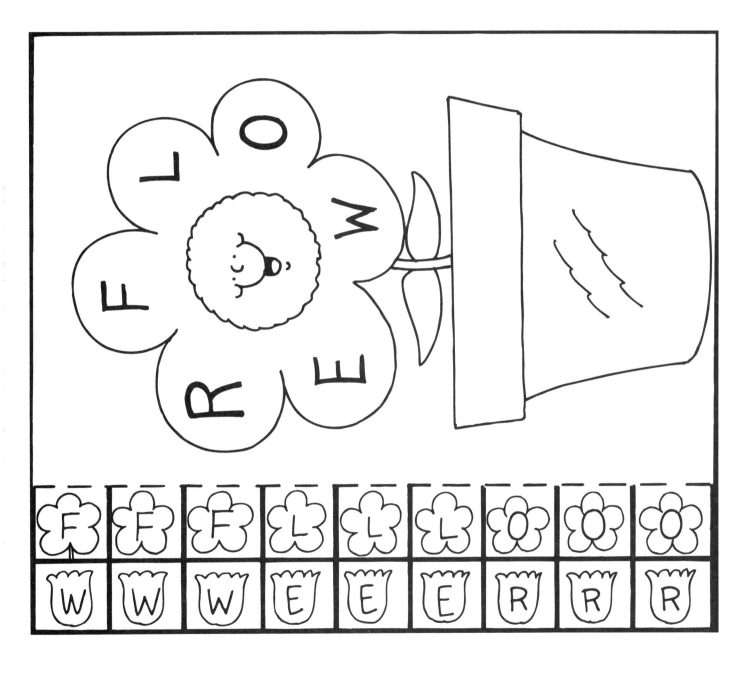

SS48838

Lovable Lions

(wall hanging) Daniel 6

Our God is a God of miracles! The Bible tells numerous, true stories that confirm this. This craft ties in with the story of Daniel. Because he would only worship God and not the king, Daniel was sentenced to a terrible punishment. Daniel was placed into a den filled with ferocious lions. Everyone thought he would be quickly eaten by them. But God caused the lions to be as harmless as tiny kittens! Daniel remained safe and was released. Always remember that this same God can work miracles in our lives, too!

Materials Needed:

three metal juice can lids; pink, red, brown, and black felt and/or construction paper; yellow and orange yarn; one soda pop tab; 2" x 12" piece of satin ribbon; black fine-tip marker; glue; scissors

Directions:

1. Use brown felt or construction paper to cover two of the lids to make lion faces. Continue to use felt, construction paper, and the fine-tip marker to create their faces. Make them look happy. Let dry.

2. Glue small lengths of orange and yellow yarn onto the lids to make fluffy manes for the lions. Let dry.

3. Use pink felt or construction paper to cover the remaining lid. Continue to use felt, construction paper, and the fine-tip marker to create Daniel's face, hair, and beard. Let dry.

4. Lay the completed lids, evenly spaced, onto the ribbon. Glue them into place. Let dry.

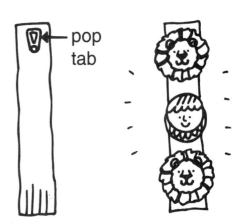

pop tab

5. Position the soda pop tab behind the top of the ribbon as shown and glue in place. This will serve as the hanger. Let dry.

6. Hang your masterpiece in a place where you can admire it and often remember the story of "Daniel and the Lions."

12

SS48838

Furnace of Fire

(pencil holder) Daniel 3

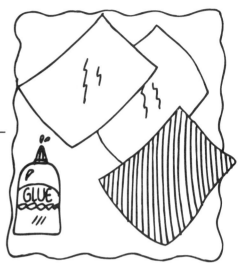

Shadrach, Meshach, and Abednego were three men that God saved. Their ruler, King Nebuchadnezzar, had made a huge idol and commanded that everyone worship it. Shadrach, Meshach, and Abednego worshipped God, and they refused to do this. Therefore, they were thrown into a furnace of fire. But when the king looked in, he saw the most amazing sight! Shadrach, Meshach, Abednego, and a fourth figure—an angel of the Lord— were walking around in perfect condition. This convinced King Nebuchadnezzar that God was real! He called for the three courageous men to come out of the fire. Once out, they were found to be unharmed. After this, the king wanted everyone to worship God, not the idol. Make the pencil holder below to remind you of this remarkable miracle!

Materials Needed:

glass jar (medium-sized); red, yellow, and orange tissue paper; four new pencils with erasers; black fine-tip marker; shallow bowl; spoon; water; glue; scissors

Directions:

1. Cut the tissue paper into 1" x 1" squares.

2. Put some glue and water into the bowl. Stir with a spoon until you have a runny mixture.

3. Dip the tissue paper squares into the glue mixture and place them onto the jar, overlapping their edges. Continue doing this until the entire outside of the jar is covered. This jar will now represent the fiery furnace. Let everything dry.

4. Use the black marker to draw smiling faces onto the erasers on the pencils as shown. They will be symbols of the four men in the furnace. Sharpen the pencils and place them in the jar where the whole family will be able to use them.

13

SS48838

Sing a Song for God

(songs)

What's God Like?

We can know what God is like through the life of Jesus. He was and always will be the only sinless human that ever lived. This song will help you think of and explore the many, wonderful qualities that Jesus displayed during His time on earth.

Sing the words below to the tune of "This Old Man." When you come to the line with a * by it, insert the word "merciful." Then the next time you sing the song and you come to this line, point to someone. That someone will then need to say one word that describes Jesus. Continue to do this until everyone has had a turn.

What's God like?

We want to know.

What did Jesus Christ's life show?

*He is (insert word given by last chosen child).

Yes, He is. That's true.

Now it's time that we ask you (point to someone).

All-Powerful and All-Knowing

God is the most powerful and knowledgeable being that ever has or ever will exist. There is nothing He can't do. There is nothing He doesn't know. Praise Him by singing the song below!

Sing the words below to the tune of "This Land Is My Land." Before you begin, look around and see if you can find a simple item that can be used as an instrument. You could tap a pencil, click two spoons together, or shake a set of keys!

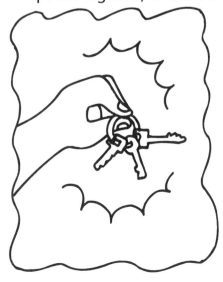

God is all-powerful,

And He's all-knowing,

When the sun is shining,

Or the wind is blowing.

When there is trouble,

We need not worry—

God's in control of everything!

14

SS48838

Love Letters

(stamps)

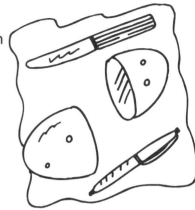

Do you know what the Bible is like? It's like a love letter that God wrote to each one of us. It is filled with everything we need to know in this life. If we follow its teachings, we can have peace, joy, comfort, and most importantly, we can spend all of eternity with God Himself, because of His Son, Jesus. Do you like writing letters? Create some stamps of your own so you can decorate one of your very own letters.

Materials Needed:

one firm potato (cut in half), table knife, washable ink pad, piece of white typing paper, envelope, paper towels, pencil, pen

Directions:

1. Use the table knife to carve a shape or design that will stand out from the flat areas on your potato halves as shown, or have an adult help you with this.

2. When your potato stamps are finished, use a paper towel to wipe off the excess moisture. Then press your stamp down firmly onto the ink pad and wiggle it side to side.

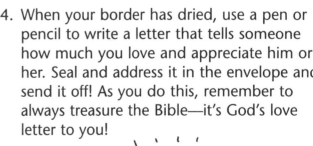

3. Stamp around the edges of your paper to create a border. You may want to alternate stamp designs or do one of each on opposite sides—it's up to you!

4. When your border has dried, use a pen or pencil to write a letter that tells someone how much you love and appreciate him or her. Seal and address it in the envelope and send it off! As you do this, remember to always treasure the Bible—it's God's love letter to you!

15

SS48838

Made to Shine

(star)

God inspired men to write down the words that would make up the Bible. He gave them the ideas and thoughts they needed. When we read God's Word, it should give us ideas of ways we can show Jesus' love to others. Get ready to create a lovely star that can "inspire" you to shine for Jesus!

Materials Needed:

star pattern
piece of tagboard (a little larger than the star pattern)
burnt matches
glue
scissors

Directions:

1. Cut out the star pattern and glue it onto the tagboard. Let it dry.

2. Cut away the extra tagboard surrounding your star.

3. Carefully glue the burnt matches to your star in a pattern similar to the one shown. Notice that some of the matches will need to be broken.

4. Place your completed star in a place where you will see it each day when you wake up!

16

SS48838

Keep Us Safe

(place mat)

The devil and many people would like to destroy the Bible. But God has protected it in such a way that this could never happen. We can be thankful and praise Him for this! Make the place mat below that will be protected in a special way so that the picture on it will stay safe—just like the Bible!

Materials Needed:

large sheet of white construction paper
pastel crayons
clear, adhesive film or a laminator

Directions:

1. Draw a scene on the white paper that symbolizes protection and safety to you. It could be a bird in a birdhouse, your home, your parents, etc.

2. When you are finished, give it to your teacher. He or she will then place and press down a clear film onto the front and back of your picture or put it through a laminator.

3. Use your picture as a place mat at meals. You won't need to worry if you spill because the clear film is protecting it. You can use a wet rag and wipe it off. When you clean your place mat, thank God that He has protected the Bible for us!

17

Turn Over Turtle

(paperweight)

It's so good to know that the Bible will never be done away with. We know this because God has promised to protect it! As you work on creating the turtle paperweight below, stop and think about the way this creature is protected. Whenever it senses danger, it simply pulls its head, legs, and tail inside its hard shell. What terrific protection God has provided for turtles—and for our beloved Bible!

Materials Needed:

medium-size rock with a flat bottom, green acrylic paint, paintbrush, gold paint pen, black fine-tip marker, green felt, glue, scissors

Directions:

1. Place your rock on a flat surface, bottom down, and paint it green to look like a turtle's shell. Let it dry.

2. Cut a head, four legs, and a tail from the felt. Glue these pieces to the bottom edges of the rock. Be careful to leave plenty of room for writing later. Let it dry.

3. Use the black marker to create two eyes on the head and webbed feet on the legs as shown.

4. Flip your turtle over. Use the gold paint pen to write "The Bible can't be destroyed" on the bottom of the turtle.

5. Use your turtle as a paperweight and read its message often.

18

SS48838

Bible Box

(trinket holder)

There are sixty-six separate books in the Bible. Each has its own name and contains chapters and individual verses. When they are all combined together, they become one big book—the Bible! Here's a craft that can remind us of this awesome fact!

Materials Needed:

small rectangular box with no lid, piece of cardboard—a little larger than the bottom of the box, masking tape, black and white construction paper, small square of red construction paper, black fine-tip marker, red marker, silver paint pen, glue, scissors, pencil

Directions:

1. Place the box, bottom down, onto the cardboard. Use a pencil to trace around it. Carefully cut this out.

2. Tape the cardboard onto the box as shown to create a lid that opens and closes like the cover of a book.

3. Glue black construction paper to cover the left side, lid, and bottom of the box. Let dry.

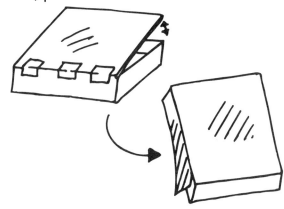

4. Glue white construction paper to cover the three remaining sides. Let dry.

5. Use the black marker to draw horizontal lines on the white sides. This will create the look of pages.

6. Use the silver pen to write "Holy Bible" on the top of the lid as shown.

7. Use the red marker to write a large 66 on the inside bottom of the box.

8. Cut out a small red construction paper cross and glue it beneath the title.

9. Your box should now look like a Bible. Use it to keep change, notes, or small trinkets in. Whenever you open it, be reminded of how many books are in the Bible!

19

Sixty-Six Books

(song)

Sixty-six books is a lot, isn't it? That's how many there are in the very best book of all, the Bible! Some of the books are short, some are long, and some are in-between, but each is very important. If even one book was missing, the Bible wouldn't be complete. What a wonderful thing God did when He gave us the Bible! Sing the song below to remind you to be thankful that we live in a place where we are allowed the freedom to read His Word whenever we want!

Sing the words below to the tune of "Jesus Loves Me." Follow the italicized instructions and illustrations to make the hand motions that accompany them.

Sixty-six books equal one.   *(Put up pointer finger of right hand.)*

God's Word was complete and done.   *(Open both hands, palms up, like an open book.)*

From our Father, they all came.   *(Wave your right hand above your head.)*

And the Bible is its name.   *(Open both hands, palms up, like an open book.)*

Let's all be thankful.   *(Place hands in a praying position and leave them like this for the next two lines.)*

Let's all be thankful.

Let's all be thankful,

For God's almighty Word.   *(Raise up left hand and make a fist to show power.)*

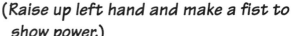

20

                                    SS48838

Ring the Right One

(game)

Do you wonder how the world came to be? Was the entire world really flooded at one time? You can find the answers to these questions and many more in God's Word—the Bible. In this game, you will have the opportunity to score points when you toss rings onto clothespins marked "Bible." It is fun and will help remind you to read the Bible to learn all about God's Word!

Materials Needed:

foam rectangular block, six clothespins (not the spring type), black fine-tip marker, toilet paper tube, ruler, scissors

Directions:

1. Use the marker to write "Bible" on three of the clothespins.

2. Arrange and push all six of the clothespins into the block as shown to make a game board. Make sure you allow enough room for a toilet paper ring to fit over and between each clothespin.

3. Use the ruler and marker to mark every half inch on the toilet paper tube. Carefully cut on the marks to create nine small rings.

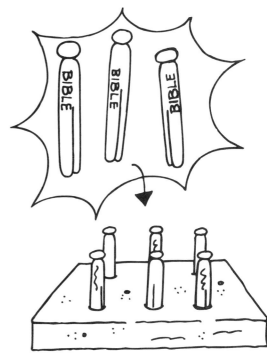

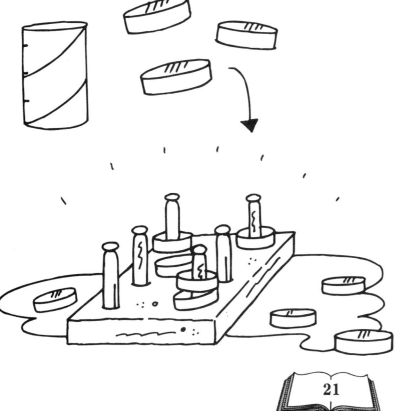

4. Place your assembled game board on the floor. Stand or kneel on the seat of a chair (with the back in front of you).

5. Take aim and try to drop your rings onto the pins that are marked "Bible." You score five points for every ring that does.

6. Play by yourself or challenge a friend to beat your score. Whoever wins gets to pick a favorite Bible story to read.

21

SS48838

Beaker of Bibles

(word search)

When we read about historical or scientific things in the Bible, we can know without a doubt that they are true. You may hear ideas that go against what God's Word says, but don't believe them for a second! The Bible is always right and trustworthy.

The word "Bible" is hidden inside the beaker below thirteen times. Look carefully—it may be spelled forward, backward, up, down, or diagonally. Circle each "Bible" that you find with a highlighter marker.

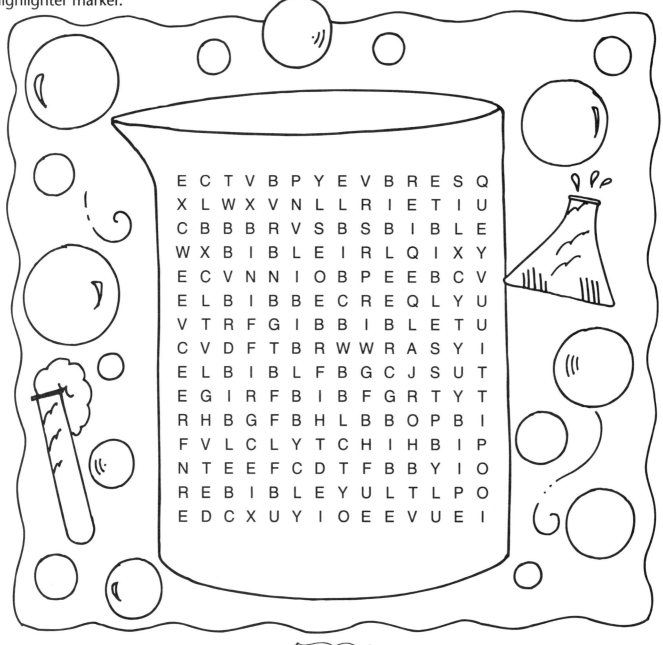

```
E C T V B P Y E V B R E S Q
X L W X V N L L R I E T I U
C B B B R V S B S B I B L E
W X B I B L E I R L Q I X Y
E C V N N I O B P E E B C V
E L B I B B E C R E Q L Y U
V T R F G I B B I B L E T U
C V D F T B R W W R A S Y I
E L B I B L F B G C J S U T
E G I R F B I B F G R T Y T
R H B G F B H L B B O P B I
F V L C L Y T C H I H B I P
N T E E F C D T F B B Y I O
R E B I B L E Y U L T L P O
E D C X U Y I O E E V U E I
```

22

SS48838

Becoming Better

(hanging butterfly)

When we study God's Word and put it to use, we become better people and more pleasing to God. The Bible tells us that if we accept Jesus as our Savior (ask Him to forgive our sins and believe that He died on the cross for us), we become born again. This is a wonderful change because it means we can be sure that when we die, we will go to heaven to live with God! We are like a caterpillar that, by God's grace, has been changed into a butterfly that can soar into freedom. Get set to make your own butterfly with any wing designs you wish!

Materials Needed:

butterfly wings pattern on page 24, construction paper, one clothespin (not the spring type), two 1/4" x 1 1/2" strips of black construction paper, black fine-tip marker, variety of decorative materials (buttons, stickers, aluminum foil, glitter, yarn, crayons, etc.), pencil, string, glue, scissors

Directions:

1. Cut out the pattern.

2. Place it on a piece of construction paper and use a pencil to trace around it. Cut it out.

3. Decorate the wings by gluing on any of the materials provided. (Some ideas are provided on page 24.)

4. While the wings dry, use the black marker to draw a face onto the ball of the clothespin as shown. This will be the butterfly's head.

5. Fold the ends of the construction paper strips about 1/4" from one end. Glue these ends onto the top of the head for antennae. Let dry.

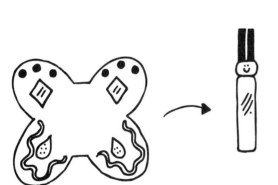

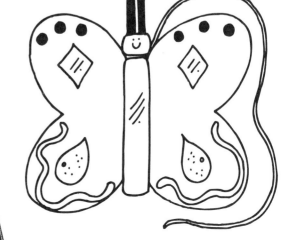

6. Put a long line of glue down the back of the clothespin. Firmly press it onto the wings as shown.

7. Let your butterfly dry.

8. Tie a length of string around its neck so you can hang it.

23

SS48838

Becoming Better

(hanging butterfly) continued

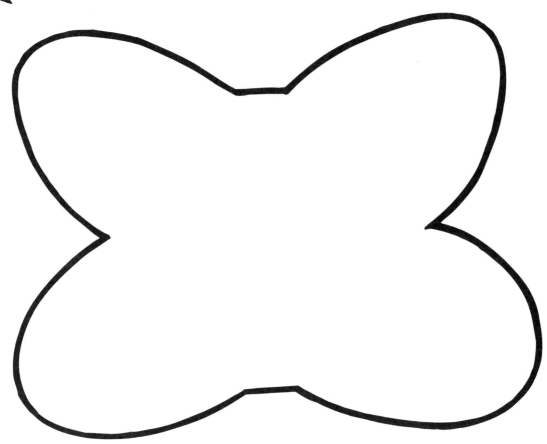

Decorating Ideas

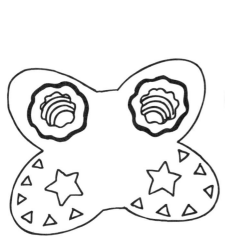

24

SS48838

He Is a Spirit

(wind chime)

God's Word teaches us that God is a spirit. Even though we can't see Him, we can be sure He is always there. Stop and think about all the things that we can't see and yet know that they exist. We can't see electricity, but it is there to light bulbs, cook things on the stove, or help us blow dry our hair. And think about the wind. Even though it is invisible, we can see the leaves it blows and the kite it keeps up in the sky. Make a wind chime that will help remind you that God is a spirit!

Materials Needed:

plastic coffee can lid (medium or large), four metal juice lids, hole punch, masking tape, ruler, string, construction paper, markers, glue, scissors

Directions:

1. Punch four holes, evenly spaced, around the edge of the coffee can lid as shown.

2. Cut four 8" lengths of string. Thread and tie each through a hole on the lid.

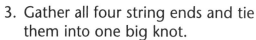

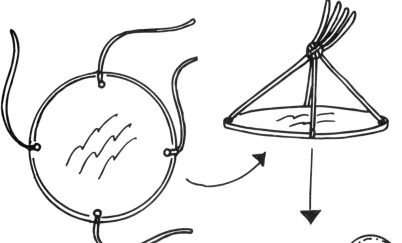

3. Gather all four string ends and tie them into one big knot.

4. Cut and glue construction paper to cover the front side of each of the juice lids. Use markers to decorate around the edges. Write the word "He" on the first lid, "is" on the second, "with" on the third, and "us" on the last.

5. Cut four more 8" lengths of string. Tape one end of each to the backs of the lids.

6. Thread the other ends of the string through the holes on the coffee can lid. Try to have the backs face one another.

7. Hang your wind chime from a hook or hanging string!

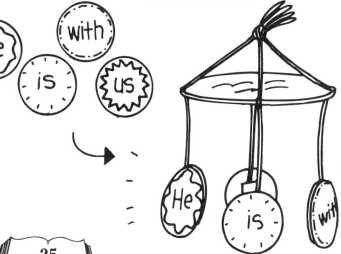

25

SS48838

A Personal Being

(game)

Did you know that God is a personal being? He wants you to spend time with Him, just like you do with your friends. When you spend time with God, by praying or reading His Word, you can get to know Him better! The game below is fun to play with your friends—and one that your Heavenly Father will enjoy watching!

Materials Needed:

one stopwatch (for the whole group)

Directions:

1. Choose someone to be the "actor" and someone to operate the stopwatch. The actor will need to silently think of an activity that he or she enjoys doing with a friend. It could be jumping rope, skateboarding, riding a bike, playing video games, etc.

2. Once the actor has an idea in mind, he or she shouts, "Go." This will signal that the stopwatch should be started.

3. The actor has one minute to silently act out the chosen activity. During this minute, all of the players are welcome to yell out guesses. If someone guesses correctly, this person and the actor both get one point. If no one guesses, then no points are awarded. Either way, the actor only gets one chance.

4. Let everyone take a turn. Whoever ends up with the most points is the winner!

26

SS48838

We're in God's Hands

(photo album)

Have you ever heard that God is eternal? This means that He will go on and on forever. Did you know that God is everywhere all at once? These things can be a bit hard to understand, but once you understand these things, you can be assured that God will never leave you. You don't need to worry that God will die or that you will go some place where His loving eyes can't follow. Make the photo album below to remind you that God loves all of us and He always will.

Materials Needed:

hand patterns on page 28, crayons, two brads, a small picture of yourself, typing paper, pencil, glue, scissors

Directions:

1. Color the words on the hand pattern. Cut both hands out.

2. Glue your picture under the words on the hand as shown.

3. Place the blank hand onto the typing paper and use a pencil to trace around it several times. Cut all the hands out.

4. Place all the blank hands so that they line up behind the hand with your picture on it.

5. Poke the brads through the black dots and through all of the hand pages.

6. Take your new photo album home. Glue or tape pictures of your family and friends in it. Write their names below the pictures. As you do this, remember that God is eternal and can see each one of us!

SS48838

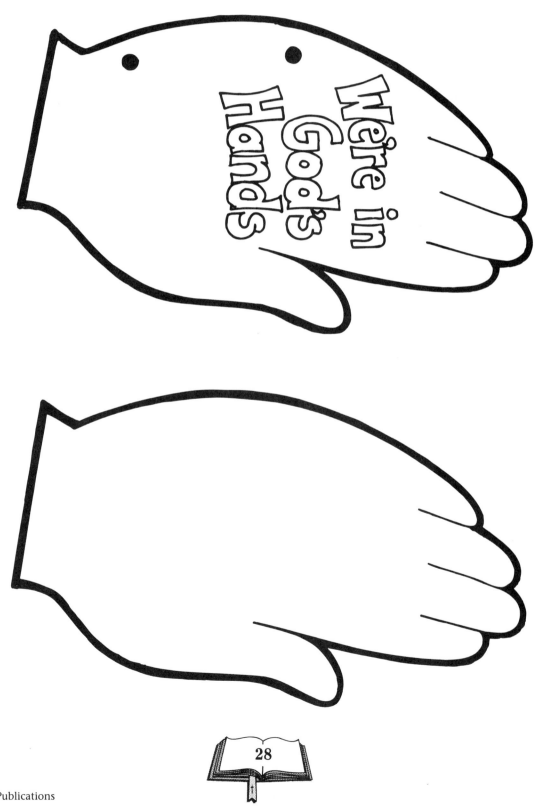

We're in God's Hands

SS48838

Holy and Just

(shepherd and sheep figures)

We can be thankful that God is holy—that He is only good and there is no evil in Him. He is also a fair God. We are very fortunate that He wants to be like a shepherd to us. God wants to lead, guide, and help us through this life. Therefore, we can think of ourselves as His sheep. We need to follow and listen to Him. Make a shepherd and a sheep to remind yourself of these things.

Materials Needed:

shepherds and sheep patterns on page 30, one empty juice can, one half of a toilet paper tube, facial tissue, rubber band, yarn, white construction paper, large paper clip, tape, small piece of gray felt, crayons, glue, scissors

Directions (shepherd):

1. Color and cut out the shepherd's face and arms patterns.

2. Use glue and construction paper to cover the bottom two-thirds of the juice can as shown.

3. Glue on the shepherd's face.

4. Cover the top of the can with the center of the facial tissue. Use scissors to trim away the tissue from the shepherd's face. Place a rubber band around the top of the can to create a head covering. Trim the edges of the covering.

5. Fold back the tabs on the arm pieces. Glue the tabs to the body.

6. As a finishing touch, use yarn to make a belt for the shepherd's garment.

Directions (sheep):

1. Color and cut out the sheep's head pattern.

2. Tape the paper clip to the back as shown.

3. Use glue and construction paper to cover the toilet paper tube.

4. Clip the head onto the tube as shown.

5. Cut four small rectangles from the gray felt. Glue them onto the tube to serve as feet.

6. Not everyone knows that God longs to be their shepherd. You can use your shepherd and sheep figures to help explain this!

back

29

SS48838

Holy and Just

(shepherd and sheep patterns) continued

30

SS48838

Greatest Gift of Love

(yarn cross)

God sent us the greatest gift ever when He sent His only Son, Jesus, to be born on earth. When Jesus grew up, He willingly suffered and died on a cross. He became the perfect sacrifice that would allow forgiveness for all our wrongdoing. Three days later, Jesus came back to life. When we believe in and accept what Jesus did and ask Him to forgive us for our sins, Jesus "saves" us. This means we will spend eternity with God after we die! Because of all this, the cross has become a powerful symbol. Make your own cross that will help you share its important message!

Materials Needed:

"Jesus Died for You" pattern (below), 1" x 7" strip of cardboard, 1" x 5" strip of cardboard, yarn, duct tape, glue, scissors

Directions:

1. Cut out and glue the "Jesus Died for You" pattern onto the 7" strip of cardboard, 2" down from the top.

2. Glue the 5" strip to the back of the 7" strip, to form a cross, as shown.

3. Cut a small slit in the top right corner of the 7" strip.

4. Place the end of a piece of yarn into the slit. Knot the end to secure it in place.

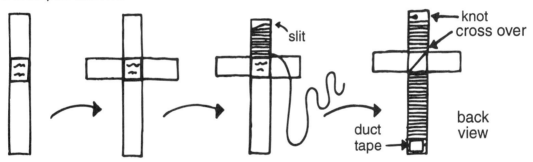

5. Now wind the yarn around and around the whole strip. You can use one color, or you can tie several different ones together. Cross over the back as shown so you don't cover the pattern. When finished, use duct tape to tape down the end of the yarn in back.

6. Cut another small slit in the top left corner of the 5" strip.

7. Repeat steps 4 and 5 to cover the whole strip.

8. Proudly place your cross where others will notice it. Get ready to explain its meaning!

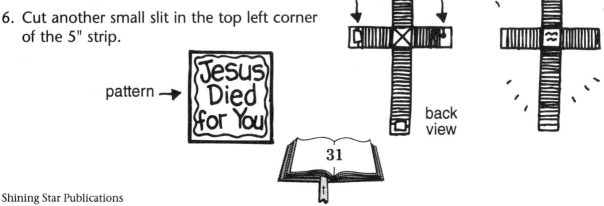

31

SS48838

Unique Universe

(centerpiece)

One of God's most spectacular creations is the universe! He not only made the earth we live on— but all other planets and stars as well! Would you like to arrange stars and planets? Here is your chance!

Materials Needed:

patterns on page 33, square foam block, pipe cleaners, soda pop tabs, acrylic paints, paintbrushes, small foam balls, glitter and sequins, newspaper, masking tape, glue, scissors, crayons

Directions:

1. Paint the foam balls. They will be your planets. Let dry.

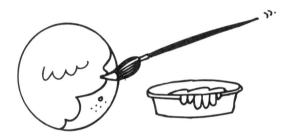

2. Color the sun, moon, and star shapes on page 33. Cut them out. To add extra dazzle, smear them with glue and sprinkle glitter or sequins on them. Gently shake the excess onto newspaper. Let dry.

3. Poke and push pipe cleaners down into the foam block. Bend them in all directions. Bend little hooks at the ends.

bend ¼ of pipe down

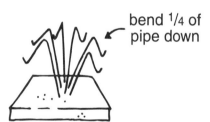

4. Push soda pop tabs down into your "planets" as shown.

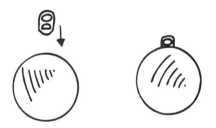

5. Tape soda pop tabs onto the backs of your sun, moon, and stars as shown.

6. Hang the completed items on the pipe cleaner hooks. When you are finished, place your lovely centerpiece on a table or shelf.

32

SS48838

Unique Universe

(centerpiece patterns) continued

SS48838

Pretty Plants

(landscaped lid)

Do you appreciate the trees, flowers, plants, and shrubs that surround us? There are so many kinds, sizes, and colors of them to admire! Our God is an awesome artist! Here's an opportunity to try to capture some of that beauty by creating a scene with some unusual painting tools!

Materials Needed:

shallow shoebox lid (medium to large), white construction paper, tempera paints (placed in shallow bowls), variety of items that can be used instead of a paintbrush (toothbrush, toothpicks, cotton swabs, craft sticks, plastic fork, etc.), yarn, newspaper, masking tape, pencil, glue, scissors

Directions:

1. Place the shoebox lid onto the white construction paper. Use the pencil to trace around it. Then cut just inside your pencil lines. Check to be sure your paper will fit neatly inside the lid, then take it out, and place it onto newspaper.

2. Use the various items provided to paint a scene on the white paper that is filled with trees, bushes, plants, flowers, etc. You could use a toothbrush to create leaves, toothpicks to make blades of grass, and cotton swabs pressed down to fashion bright flowers. Use your imagination! Let your landscape dry.

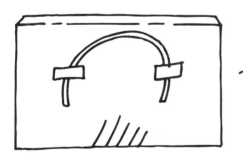

3. Use masking tape to tape a length of yarn onto the lid (not the side you'll put the picture into) to make a hanger.

4. Smear glue onto the back of your picture and press it firmly down inside the lid.

5. Hang your masterpiece where others can appreciate your talent.

34

SS48838

Clothespin Critters

(animal magnets)

What's your favorite animal? Are there too many to choose just one? They were all specially designed by God! He created every one—from the gigantic elephants to the tiniest birds. Get set to make some critters that can help out at your house by holding notes or messages!

Materials Needed:

critter patterns on page 36, a sheet of white tagboard (a little larger than the critter patterns page), four spring-type clothespins, crayons, self-adhesive magnetic strips, glue, scissors

Directions:

1. Color the animal patterns.

2. Glue the page onto the tagboard. Let dry.

3. Cut the animals out. Squeeze glue onto the dotted lines. Position and press a clothespin onto each as shown. Let dry.

4. Firmly press self-adhesive magnetic strips onto the back of your critters.

5. Put them on the refrigerator where their trunk, legs, and other body parts can hold papers for your family!

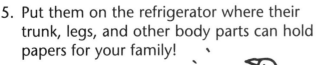

SS48838

Clothespin Critters

(animal magnet patterns) continued

36

SS48838

Man Is Marvelous

(napkin holder)

One of God's most amazing creations are humans! Stop and think about the way we're put together. He designed hearts to pump blood, fingers to pick things up, legs to bend and run, and eyes to see! Regardless of all this, the most important thing is that God made all people. He made them to be all sizes, shapes, and colors. He loves us all, and we should love each other, too! Make the napkin holder below to help you express love to your family.

Materials Needed:

medium-size box of narrow width, acrylic paints, paintbrushes, aluminum foil, six craft sticks, black fine-tip marker, yarn, tape, glue, scissors

Directions:

1. Carefully cut off the ends of your box as shown. This is your basic napkin holder.

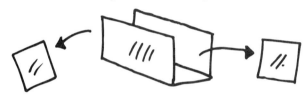

2. Tape aluminum foil to cover your holder.

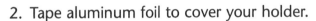

3. Glue a length of yarn onto both sides in the design shown below. Let dry.

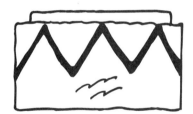

4. Paint six craft sticks the color of skin tones (pink, yellow, orange, brown, etc.). Let dry.

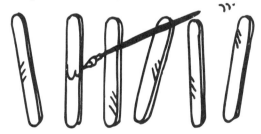

5. Use the marker to draw faces on the sticks.

6. Position and glue the craft sticks onto the holder as shown. It should appear as though your people are holding hands.

7. Use your napkin holder at the dinner table—a good place to be with those you love!

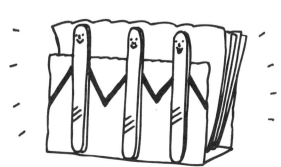

37

SS48838

God Rules Nature

(banner)

When leaves fall, flowers bloom, and baby bunnies learn to hop, we know this is all part of nature. But have you ever wondered who the force is behind all this activity? If you said God, then you're right! Because of Him, the sun and moon shine, the seasons change in exact order, and all living things continue on. Think of this as you make a felt banner that displays the wonders of nature!

Materials Needed:

blue piece of felt

dowel stick (longer than the width of the piece of felt)

decorative materials (scraps of felt, buttons, yarn, black and green fabric paint, etc.)

glue

scissors

Directions:

1. Squeeze and smear glue to make a wide strip on the edge of the blue felt as shown. Lay the dowel stick onto it and roll it completely in the felt. Let dry.

2. Use the materials provided to create a nature scene. You might use small diamond shapes of green felt to make a treetop, fabric paint for birds, and buttons for flowers. There is no right or wrong way—just have fun! Let everything dry.

3. Tie a piece of yarn onto the ends of the dowel stick to make a hanger. Ask your mom or dad if they'll display your banner in a hallway or on a wall that needs to be brightened up!

38

SS48838

He Rules Everywhere

(song)

Nations and countries all have officials who rule them. Even though these men and women hold powerful positions, there is still one who rules over them. That one is God. He is the ultimate ruler over all! Below is a song that describes this!

Sing the words to the tune of "Old MacDonald." As you do, see if you can make a clapping or snapping rhythm to accompany it. One person can lead this song while the rest follow along!

God rules over all this world.

His Word tells us so.

He's in charge, and I am glad.

And this I surely know.

He rules here, He rules there—

Ruling, ruling everywhere.

In this knowledge, we can rest

For our Father knows what's best.

Sing the songs below to the tune of "Happy Birthday." Have half the group sing while the other half whistles the tune for a neat blend.

God rules everywhere.
This message we share.
Let's never turn our backs,
On His tender care.

Don't ever forget
How much He loves you.
He'll gladly rule our lives
If we just ask Him to.

39

SS48838

All the World

(maze)

Ruling over all the world seems like an impossible job, and it would be for any human being. Men and women can only be in one place at a time. They don't know what others are thinking, and they can't be aware of everything at once. But God, on the other hand, is able to be present everywhere. He is all-knowing. He is the world's perfect ruler! As you work through the maze, silently thank Him for loving and caring for our world!

Begin at the arrow marked "start" and wind your way through the world. Exit at the arrow marked "end." When you are finished, trace over the world shape and create a maze for a friend to do.

40

God Is My Ru[ler]

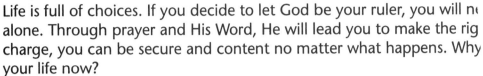

(door decoration)

Life is full of choices. If you decide to let God be your ruler, you will n[ever be]
alone. Through prayer and His Word, He will lead you to make the rig[ht choices. With God in]
charge, you can be secure and content no matter what happens. Why [not let Him take control of]
your life now?

Materials Needed:

door decoration pattern on page 42, tagboard (a little larger than the door decoration), crayons, a variety of decorative materials (flat beads, sequins, yarn, etc.), glue, scissors

Directions:

1. Glue the door decoration onto the tagboard. Let dry.

2. Carefully cut it out. Cut along the dotted lines, too.

3. Color the words and the background.

4. Glue on any of the materials provided to make your decoration more attractive. Beads or sequins would look nice on the crown, while yarn or twine could be added onto the border design. Let everything dry.

5. If you haven't already, make the decision to let God rule your life by accepting Jesus Christ as your Savior. Hang the door decoration on a doorknob at home. Each time you leave the room, you will be reminded of the wonderful commitment you have made!

41

SS48838

God Is My Ruler

(door decoration pattern) continued

SS48838

Count on God

(game)

Because God is always present and available to each of us, we can count on Him to help us through our day. No matter what we find ourselves in need of, we should always turn to Him first. He loves us and knows what is best. Get set to play a game that will help us remember to depend on God!

Materials Needed:

long piece of butcher paper, black broad-tipped marker, yardstick, three paper plates, paper, pencil

Directions:

1. Use the marker and yardstick to divide the paper into 15, equal-sized (larger than a paper plate), and numbered squares as shown. This will be the scoreboard.

2. Mark a capital "G" on the first plate, "O" on the next, and "D" on the last to spell out "God."

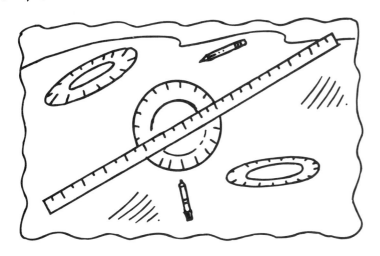

3. Let each player take a turn tossing the plates (one at a time) onto the scoreboard. If a plate lands completely inside a square, the player receives that number of points. Use the pencil and paper to keep score.

4. Whoever ends up with the most points wins!

43

                                                                                      SS48838

Praising His Power

(game)

God is all-powerful! There is nothing that God cannot do. The Bible is filled with stories that remind us of this. The world around us also reinforces this. Spend a few minutes thinking of examples that demonstrate God's awesome power. Then join in a game that will give you the opportunity to share your thoughts on God's power with others!

Materials Needed:

"P" pattern on page 45, tagboard, decorative materials (sequins, glitter, stickers, etc.), glue, scissors, stopwatch

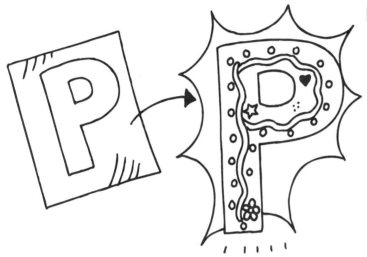

Directions:

1. Glue the "P" pattern onto tagboard. Let it dry and cut it out.

2. Use glue and the materials provided to decorate it. Let it dry.

3. Have players sit in a circle and appoint someone to hold the decorated "P."

4. Next, choose a timekeeper (a non-player) to operate the stopwatch. The timekeeper should start the watch and yell, "Praise His Power," as the signal to begin. At this time, the players should begin passing the "P" around the circle.

5. After 30 seconds, the timekeeper should again shout, "Praise His Power." This signals that the passing should stop.

6. Whoever is holding the "P" should then stand. The stopwatch should be started again. The standing child says, "P is for Power! I know God is powerful because . . ." The player should then finish this sentence with his or her own idea. (Examples: "I know God is powerful because He divided the Red Sea so the Israelites could pass through it." Or, "I know God is powerful because He raised Jesus up from death." Or, "I know God is powerful because He is the force that keeps my heart beating.")

7. If, after 30 seconds, the girl or boy cannot finish the phrase, he or she is "out."

8. Continue playing until one person is left and is proclaimed the winner!

Praising His Power

(game) continued

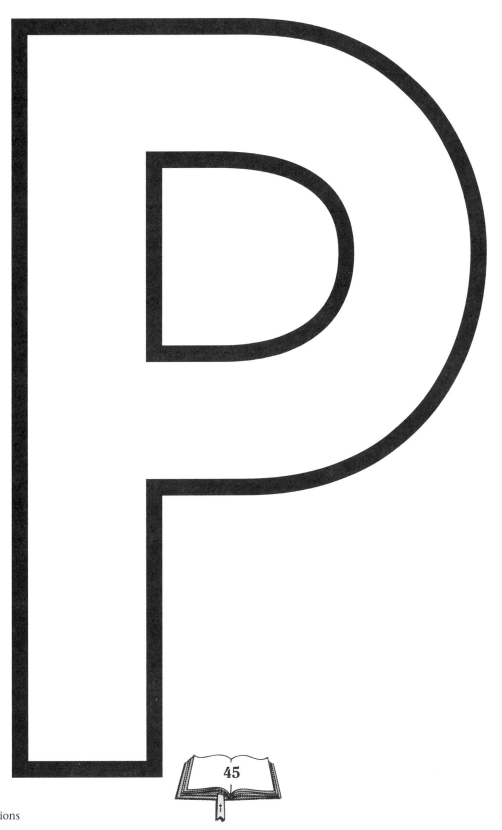

SS48838

God Knows Everything

(fish with a flap)

God knows everything that goes on. He knows every thought in our hearts and minds. This craft is a wonderful way to learn the story of Jonah and how he learned his lesson. After you make your fish, use it to help you share this story with others.

Materials Needed:

copy of "Jonah's Lesson" and the prayer on page 47, fish and Jonah patterns on page 48, crayons, glue, scissors

Directions:

1. Read "Jonah's Lesson" and the prayer on page 47. Cut them out.

2. Color the fish and Jonah patterns. Cut them out (leave Jonah in the square).

3. Cut along the dotted lines on the fish's belly. Fold the flap up on the solid line.

4. Put a line of glue around the top and sides of Jonah's picture. Press it onto the back of the fish so it is positioned underneath the flap as shown below. Let dry.

5. Glue "Jonah's Lesson" onto the back of the fish.

6. Find someone you want to tell the story of Jonah to. Hold up your fish and read the glued-on story. When you get to the part about the fish, lift up the flap so that your audience can see Jonah praying from inside.

7. Say the prayer from page 47 with the person you told the story of Jonah to.

Jonah's lesson

back of Jonah's picture

← flap

46

God Knows Everything

(Jonah's Lesson and prayer) continued

Jonah's Lesson

Once there was a man named Jonah. God told Jonah to go to the city of Nineveh and warn the people there to stop their sinful behavior. But Jonah didn't want to go. Instead, he foolishly thought he could run away. God, of course, knew all about his plan. And when Jonah got onto a ship, God caused a terrible storm to happen. Jonah knew God wasn't pleased with him. He told the others on the ship that they should throw him into the sea so the storm would stop. When they did, God had a huge fish swallow Jonah. For three days, Jonah lived inside the fish. During that time, Jonah prayed. He told God he was sorry and was ready to obey. The fish spit Jonah out onto the shore. Jonah had learned his lesson. He went to Nineveh and did what God wanted.

A Prayer for You

Dear God,

Thank You for Your Word that teaches us about Jonah. Please help me to always obey You—even when it is very hard. Please help me also to remember that You have a plan for my life. I know You love me and want what's best for me. Help me be an example of obedience for others. Amen.

SS48838

God Knows Everything

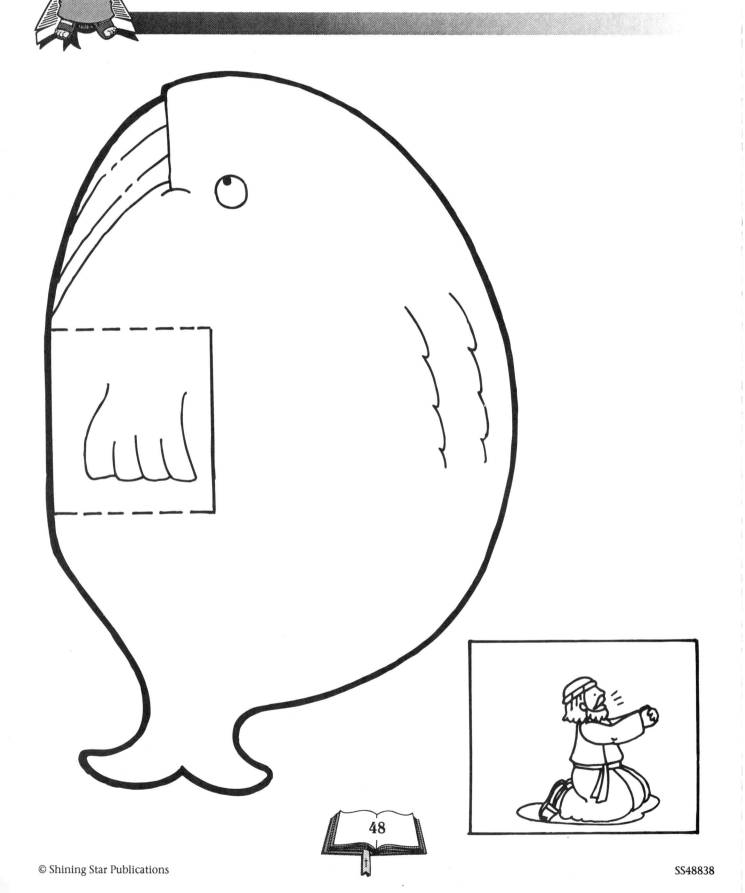

48